Remembering
Las Vegas

Jeff Burbank

TURNER
PUBLISHING COMPANY

Early visitors would never have believed Nevada's rugged landscape would give birth to a dazzling city of lights, gambling, and entertainment, famous around the world.

Remembering
Las Vegas

Turner Publishing Company
www.turnerpublishing.com

Remembering Las Vegas

Copyright © 2010 Turner Publishing Company

Library of Congress Control Number: 2010924309

ISBN: 978-1-59652-653-2

Printed in the United States of America

ISBN: 978-1-68336-847-2 (pbk.)

CONTENTS

In the late 1930s to 1940s, the dealer of a roulette game at the Apache bar on Fremont Street pushes stacks of casino chips toward a winning gambler.

ACKNOWLEDGMENTS

This volume, *Remembering Las Vegas,* is the result of the cooperation and efforts of many individuals and organizations. It is with great thanks that we acknowledge the valuable contribution of the University of Nevada Las Vegas Libraries, Special Collections, for their generous support.

We would also like to thank Peter Michel, Director, University of Nevada Las Vegas Libraries, Special Collections, for valuable contributions and assistance in making this work possible.

———————

This project represents countless hours of review and research. The researchers and writer have reviewed thousands of photographs. We greatly appreciate the generous assistance of the archives listed here, without whom this project could not have been completed.

The goal in publishing the work is to provide broader access to a set of extraordinary photographs. The aim is to inspire, provide perspective, and evoke insight that might assist officials and citizens, who together are responsible for determining Las Vegas' future. In addition, the book seeks to preserve the past with respect and reverence.

With the exception of touching up imperfections that have accrued with the passage of time and cropping where necessary, no changes have been made. The focus and clarity of many images are limited to the technology and the ability of the photographer at the time they were recorded.

We encourage readers to reflect as they explore Las Vegas and stroll along its streets. It is the publisher's hope that in making use of this work, longtime residents will learn something new and that new residents will gain a perspective on where Las Vegas has been, so that each can contribute to its future.

—*Todd Bottorff, Publisher*

PREFACE

The photographs in this book are organized into four chronological sections. The first section, "Rise of a Railroad Boom Town," covers the founding years of Las Vegas, 1904 to 1910, from before the 1905 land auction that formed the town to the launch of the railroad through town and the creation of Clark County in 1909. The images depict the will and pioneer spirit of the early settlers at a time when they had to survive day-to-day in a sparse, desert environment that is alternately hot and cold. They reveal how rapidly both the McWilliams and Clark town sites were built so that the residents could begin their new lives, and how those residents coped as a community under harsh, crude living conditions.

The second section, "Before Hoover Dam: Molding a Desert Community," includes pictures taken in the years 1911 to 1929, during which Las Vegas began to mature as an incorporated city with stores, parks, schools, banks, and paved streets. Residents would later experience the loss of much of their railroad supply business, but in the 1920s they experienced elation when the U.S. government decided to build the Hoover Dam project, which guaranteed the city's future expansion and prosperity.

The crucial decade of the 1930s is key to the third section, "Hoover Dam, Gaming, and the Early Las Vegas Strip," covering 1930 to 1949. In the 1930s, Hoover Dam was completed, Nevada legalized casinos, the federal government ended Prohibition, and Las Vegas truly began to take off as a relaxing spot for tourists to visit on their way to see the famous, spectacular new dam. The group of photos also reveals how Las Vegas looked in the 1940s, when military spending during World War II brought another economic boom, and the first resorts were established on the fledgling Las Vegas Strip between 1941 and 1948.

Finally, in "Modern Las Vegas Takes Shape," from 1950 to 1959, the images take a brief look at the progress the city and county made during the resort boom of the 1950s, its contribution to—and benefits from—the Cold War, and the amazing growth of its visitor economy, which set up the incredible population growth and development that would come in later decades.

The Las Vegas shown in these photographs brings to light the city's changing scenery, its many booms versus few busts, and the evolution of what became the largest city in the United States to be entirely created and developed during the twentieth century.

—Jeff Burbank

Members of a railroad survey party, wearing sombreros, pose in 1904 beneath trees at the Stewart Ranch, owned by Las Vegas pioneer Helen Stewart, who in 1902 sold most of her two-thousand-acre property to William Clark, a U.S. senator from Montana. In 1905, Clark would bring in rail service and subdivide Stewart's ranch to create what today is downtown Las Vegas.

Rise of a Railroad Boom Town

(1904–1910)

The desolate center of the McWilliams town site, as it appeared in 1905, was Las Vegas' first settlement, started in 1904, about six months before the Clark Las Vegas town site. Its wooden and tent structures would be devastated by fire later in 1905.

I. W. Botkin's men's clothing business was one of the first stores to open on Fremont Street in the Clark Las Vegas town site. Botkin had originally operated at the 1904 McWilliams town site, but like many merchants, moved to Clark's in mid-1905 to be near the new railroad depot. The Palace Hotel can be seen in the background to the right and early tent houses to the left.

Banking and refreshments had to share space in the quickly built and hot confines of the original McWilliams town site in early 1905. The First State Bank stood in the heart of the McWilliams site, immediately beside the post office and a small shop, Kuhn's Merchantile. In a matter of months, most of the businesses would move southeast to the nearby Clark Las Vegas town site to be near the new rail station.

At perhaps the height of activity in the McWilliams site in early 1905, a crowd mills in the center of town outside the First State Bank and Kuhn's Merchantile. Signs selling snacks and sandwiches beside the bank reveal the boom town atmosphere.

Employees of the San Pedro, Los Angeles & Salt Lake City Railroad stand beside the engine of the historic first train to arrive in Las Vegas from Salt Lake City, in May 1905, when the tracks were finally completed following years of harsh building conditions in the Southern Nevada desert. John Charles Fremont, the train's engineer, is standing second from left.

Baggage-carrying new arrivals debark between passenger and freight cars from the first public train to arrive in Las Vegas from Los Angeles, on May 15, 1905. Among the passengers who would settle in the Clark Las Vegas town site was Ed Von Tobel, Sr., who would start a lumber business and a local family dynasty.

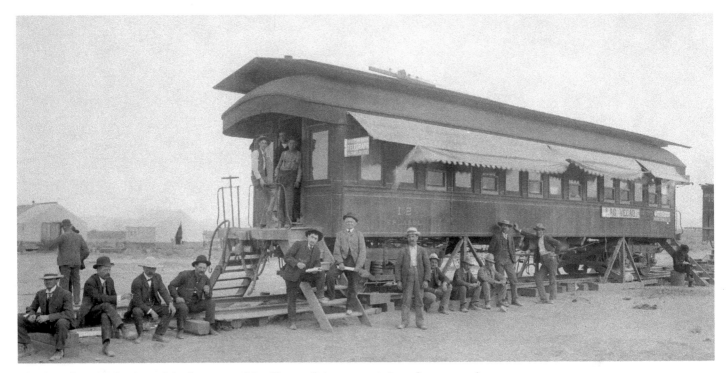

The first photograph taken of the "temporary" Las Vegas rail depot, consisting of a converted passenger car of the San Pedro, Los Angeles, and Salt Lake Railroad and some makeshift stairs, in 1905.

The rebuilt rail car serving as the Las Vegas depot soon took on a life of its own, with a ticket office and waiting room with shades over the windows in 1905. The building to the left housed offices of the Pacific Fruit Express Company and Western Union Telegraph (wire pole is seen above depot), where Joe Keat was the town's first telegraph operator.

The new Clark town site in 1905 initially permitted alcohol and prostitution on only Block 16 and 17 and soon restricted them to just Block 16, in the town's extreme northeast corner. It did not take long for Block 16 to become a bustling attraction in Las Vegas for residents and tired train passengers, with wooden saloons like the Gem, the Arizona Club, Red Onion Club, and the Arcade on the east side of North First Street between Ogden and Stewart streets. The Arizona Club would establish itself for years as the finest and fanciest saloon in town.

Lumber, cement, and other building materials, offered here at the Las Vegas Trading Company in 1905, were scarce in Clark's young town. Demand for wood was so high even the new railroad could not deliver enough to meet it. Lumber sellers bore the brunt of many complaints from residents. Carpenters received double the wages of day laborers. Many residents who arrived in 1904 and 1905 lived in portable tent houses (easily picked up and moved on wagons), and some placed pieces of lumber on the ground to serve as walkways.

The Las Vegas town site's first bakery, Vegas Home Bakery, was another refugee from the McWilliams town in 1905. It took longer to relocate than other merchants' shops because of its heavy ovens.

Progress—and spectacle—arrived quickly in the opening year of the Clark Las Vegas town site. Members of a Scottish kilt band in this 1905 parade were likely among recent arrivals brought by the new San Pedro, Los Angeles & Salt Lake City Railroad. More evidence of swift advancement is seen here in the line of structures and the wooden sidewalk along Main Street, immediately east of the rail line.

The transition from tents to more permanent buildings continued in late 1905 with this, the town's first brick building, which housed the Las Vegas Drug Store and the relocated Crowell & Abbott's General Merchandise (right). Crowell & Abbott's, formerly of the McWilliams town, installed a retractable awning. Potted palm trees decorated the outside of the building, which stood on North Main Street. One of the men outside stands next to a burro loaded with fully packed sacks.

Drivers of four-horse and six-horse teams pose outside the Arizona Club on the saloon row that was Block 16, around 1905. The bales of hay piled high in the wagons, for delivery around the region to places like Beatty and Bullfrog, served as fuel for mules and horses that were the only forms of local transportation. The drivers, with teams of up to 18 animals, weathered many hours traveling scores of miles on bumpy, dirt roads in the desert heat. Limited automobile transport, called "stages," was added in June 1905.

Main Street (running left to right, center), about 1906, included utility poles, canvas-and-wood buildings, and Las Vegas' first brick structure, the two-story Hotel Nevada. Crowell & Abbott's and the Las Vegas Drug Store are visible at far-left. In the foreground, a mule-drawn wagon is driven on a dirt road running parallel to Main Street and the railroad on the other side of Main.

For this unique view from 1906 or 1907, the photographer climbed a utility pole to take a picture of the rail yard of the San Pedro, Salt Lake City & Los Angeles Railroad, looking east toward Las Vegas. Engines traveling north and south converged here. Thirty-five of the rail line's coal-fired engines were serviced in the yard. The town's icehouse, the two-floor, wooden structure in the center, could hold up to 50 tons of frozen water, but it burned down in July 1907.

Crowds gathered beside and on the railroad to watch the Pullman passenger car carrying Montana's U.S. senator, railroad builder William A. Clark, who stopped here briefly to tout the 1905 land auction that would create modern Las Vegas. He is the namesake of Clark County, which has Las Vegas as its seat of government.

From the back of his private passenger rail car, Senator Clark addressed onlookers at the new Las Vegas town site in 1905. Although he continued to own the railroad for years, Clark never returned to Las Vegas.

Men in a longboat approach the wharf on the Colorado River at El Dorado Canyon in 1907, when the area was thought to have potential for another boom town similar to Las Vegas. Several million dollars in gold and other metals were extracted from an area centered around Nelson, about 25 miles southeast of Las Vegas, but within a few years, the mines were mostly tapped out. Some activity continued into the 1940s.

Early resident Ed Von Tobel, Sr., inspects three wagons full of heavy mining equipment and other supplies headed for the Bullfrog mining district sometime in the early 1900s. Von Tobel, formerly of Los Angeles, came to Las Vegas in 1905 and started a lumber business with partner James Beckley.

The Arizona Club, little more than a wooden shack when James O. McIntosh opened it soon after the May 1905 auction, was an immediate hit with locals. Shown here less than a year later in April 1906, following an obviously prosperous period, the two-story bar is now fashioned in a Mission building style. Built of brick and masonry, it featured red mahogany columns, leaded, beveled glass windows, front doors made of oak, a 30-foot front bar, and a back bar. McIntosh sold it to Al James in 1912, who would install a brothel upstairs.

American flags fly over the freight station of the San Pedro, Los Angeles & Salt Lake City Railroad, which set up a public area that offered shade in the summer heat on the Fourth of July, 1908.

Prehistoric petroglyphs, like these discovered in the early 1900s, were carved by the indigenous inhabitants, including the Anasazi and Paiutes, while passing through the Valley of Fire and other remote areas northeast of the Las Vegas town site over hundreds of years. The images, pounded into the heat-baked, brittle brown sandstone rock, were a form of communication through symbols, such as bighorn sheep and other animals the Indians hunted. Tribal members also used desert soil to paint images known as pictographs on rock.

Another milestone in 1905 was the first schoolhouse in Las Vegas, located in a then-isolated area on Second and Lewis streets. The wooden schoolhouse, formerly the Salt Lake Hotel, had two rooms, a potbellied stove, and one teacher. The first class in early 1905 had only a few dozen children, but by autumn the number increased to 200 students. The school was destroyed by fire in 1910.

On First Street, looking south to the intersection of Fremont Street, downtown Las Vegas had progressed as a town by the spring of 1909. It boasted many large commercial buildings and ten oiled, dirt streets with curbs. In the center is Thomas' Department Store with its wraparound sign, on the northeast corner of Fremont.

Fremont Street about 1910, west from Second Street. By then, the available space along the first two blocks of Fremont had been covered by commercial buildings.

In 1909, the original First Methodist Church was completed at Third and Bridger streets, using locally made concrete blocks. The parson's house is at right. The Methodist church, with its steeple, could be seen for miles and was one of the most noticeable buildings in town. It survives today, serving as a cafe and nightclub.

A woman relaxes with her dog on the porch of a home at the Las Vegas Ranch in the early 1900s.

Las Vegas residents gather to celebrate Labor Day outside the First State Bank at Second and Fremont streets in 1910.

An indication that automobiles had become more common in town by 1910, a traffic sign sits in the middle of Fremont Street. This image is facing west, with the train station at the end of the street.

The El Dorado Valley, a mining district southeast of Las Vegas near Arizona, about 1910.

With Sunrise Mountain in the background, about 1910 miners headed west toward Las Vegas stop their team of burros and covered wagon to check one of the animals along a dirt road.

A cowboy tends to cattle and horses on the Stewart Ranch in the early 1900s. Though she sold most of her ranch in 1902 to Clark for the Las Vegas town site, Helen J. Stewart held on to part of her tree-lined property and remained in Las Vegas until her death in 1926.

Two early Las Vegas hotels, the Union and the Shamrock, shared a building and merged into one hotel on Main Street in the early 1900s.

Bartender and hotel owner Joe Graglia stands behind the bar inside the Union Hotel, with a ceiling fan, hanging electric light, and a pool table in 1910. Spittoons line the floor in front of the bar.

In 1906, only a year after arriving in Las Vegas, Ed Von Tobel, Sr. (standing at center), with his partner, Jake Beckley (left, holding wagon reins), had built a prosperous lumber business. They opened on Main Street in 1905 but moved to this location on Fremont and First streets, which was closer to the train station. These buildings burned down in 1914, but the partners rebuilt them.

A boating crew from Las Vegas is about to make the journey to the Colorado River, about 25 miles to the southeast over rough, dirt roads in the early 1900s. Earl Rockwell is the driver, next to Henry Lutz; Pinky Waite is sitting on the burro; Frank Waite is on the first horse; Eddie Marshall is driving the buckboard; and Spud Lake is on the rear horse.

The Mission-style rail station, center, stands at the end of Fremont Street, 1909. To the left, a series of steel columns make up the partially completed machine shops of the SP, LA & SL Railroad, which served as the economic center of Las Vegas into the 1930s.

The steeple of the First Methodist Church, far right, is recognizable among structures downtown in this view facing east in 1910.

A boy stands between a rail car and the front of the American Railway Express office at the Las Vegas train station about 1908.

Packed burros are allowed to graze at the Las Vegas Ranch during a break in a business trip in the early 1900s.

BEFORE HOOVER DAM: MOLDING A DESERT COMMUNITY

(1911–1929)

Early automobiles, like this one photographed around 1912, became a more common sight after 1910, but the long trip on poor roads from anywhere to Las Vegas—almost isolated except for its railroad—was only for the sturdiest motorists and automobiles.

White-uniformed members of a parade band stand beside a group of curious children in the center of Fremont Street at First Street on Labor Day in 1914. A decorated column of the First State Bank is visible at left.

Using new technology to emphasize speed, Troy Steam Laundry offered one of the first motorized delivery services in Las Vegas in 1914. The smiling driver is Joe Dunlap, brother of Mrs. Dave Farnsworth, whose husband, Dave Farnsworth, owned the business.

On Fremont Street between First and Second streets, looking west about 1915. Automobiles had become the dominant form of transportation and servicing them at places such as the Las Vegas Garage machine shop was a big new business. With no air conditioning, driving in the open-air cars was a challenging experience in the desert summer months.

Las Vegas' first solid-built hotel, the Hotel Las Vegas, at the southeast corner of Main and Fremont, also housed this barbershop run by William J. Reid, standing at center, in 1916. This photograph was taken with the aid of a flashlight, which startled Reid's daughter, Mary (center right), who closed her eyes. In the rear is Reid's partner, George Sanderson.

People along Fremont at First Street watch as the Colossal Shows circus parades east to advertise its upcoming show, about 1916. Thomas' Department Store is visible at right.

Smoke billows from the railroad station at the end of this westerly view of Fremont Street about 1917. At left in the distance is Berkley's Mens Store, and then the Hotel Las Vegas. The First State Bank is at far-right, and across First Street is the Las Vegas Pharmacy, where Dr. Roy Martin oversaw a small hospital on the second floor.

Nurses in apron-like uniforms stand outside the San Pedro, Los Angeles & Salt Lake City railroad station in the early 1910s.

The first load of manganese ore from the Three Kids Mine several miles east of town passes the W. R. Thomas building and the Las Vegas Pharmacy on Fremont at First Street in 1917. Manganese metal was used to make bullets in both world wars. The mine operated until 1961 near what today is the Las Vegas Wash, a wetlands preserve.

Facing a large—but reversed—American flag, Las Vegas residents listen to a speech during a celebration in 1918 or 1919.

The first airplane to land in Las Vegas, a biplane, touched the ground on May 7, 1920. Regular air service, delivering mail from Los Angeles, started in 1926 at the Rockwell Airport two miles south of downtown, at a site next to the present-day Sahara Hotel.

Snowfall in 1921 covered trees, cars, and ornate, electric street lamps along Fremont Street. The Golden Hotel is at left, with the El Portal Theater across the street.

Automobiles park at angles on Fremont Street in the early 1920s.

Motorized tourists, with their dog performing atop a packed running board, pose around 1920 outside the front office of the Downtown Campground, owned by Warren Woodward, which offered budget accommodations for campers.

The First State Bank at First and Fremont streets, which would provide loans to home owners and businesses for decades, as it looked in the early 1920s.

By the 1920s, Las Vegas, with its multiple storefronts and electric street lighting, was maturing as a city, as this westerly view of the first few blocks of Fremont Street shows.

One of the first modern hotels outside the center of town, the Hotel National at 331 Carson Street was established in this two-story building and completed in 1922 by hotelier Joe Graglia.

Las Vegas auto seller James Cashman, who moved to town from Searchlight, Nevada, in 1920, set up this car dealership at the Overland Hotel, with some of his models shown here facing Main Street. Cashman's indoor showroom was around the corner, inside the Overland.

The Conklin Brothers' auto repair garage at 213 Fremont Street, advertising its fireproof, concrete block building, set up shop in the late 1910s. It specialized in servicing cars made by Ford—the largest automobile manufacturer of the time—and by Studebaker.

Dressed in a white uniform, an attendant checks a car at James Down's Texaco filling station on Fremont Street in the early 1920s.

Neon signs glitter beside street lamps at dusk as a pair of pedestrians stroll across Fremont Street in the 1920s. Prominent is the three-story Hotel Apache, the newest hotel in town. The Apache would become the site of Binion's Horseshoe three decades later.

Despite Prohibition, the nationwide ban on liquor sales from the 1920s to the early 1930s, Las Vegas was seldom short of alcoholic drinks, in part due to its remoteness from federal law enforcement. The man seen here in the early 1920s leaning against a truck at a filling station at Apex, Nevada, about ten miles northeast of Las Vegas, was reportedly a local bootlegger.

Teachers direct their grammar-school students to join hands in front of the Fifth Street Grammar School in the late 1920s. The classrooms were in the tall building in the center.

Among the automobiles showcased outside Woodard's Fireproof Garage, made of masonry on Fremont Street, is one (at left, with number 2) that may have been an early race car.

An open-air car speeds past a crowd gathered along Fremont Street in the 1920s.

The many trees that once grew on Fifth Street, at the far eastern edge of town, are seen here in the distance at the end of Fremont in the 1920s. The White Cross drugstore (at right) operated at Third and Fremont.

The driver of a truck, parked in front of a business next to the First State Bank in 1926, jokingly asks his five passengers to get off. The man at far-right with a necktie is Harley Harmon, an early Las Vegas government official.

A woman (left) walks toward the lobby of the Overland Hotel in this wide view of Fremont Street, facing east at Main Street, in the mid-1920s. The Hotel Nevada and the Northern Club are visible on the other side of the street.

Lines of shade trees cool the Overland Hotel at the corner of Main and Fremont streets in the 1920s.
The hotel provided space for salespeople to leave free samples of their wares for the public.

A bountiful crowd of people, some wearing sombreros in the bright spring sun, greet the pilot of a Western Air Express biplane—the first air mail plane to land in Las Vegas, on April 17, 1926, at the Rockwell Airport two miles south of downtown.

The Western Air Express plane service for the post office, originating in Los Angeles, started making regular deliveries to Las Vegas in 1926. It would land in Las Vegas, drop off the mail, and refuel on its way to Salt Lake City.

A woman pushing an open baby carriage prepares to cross Fremont at First Street in January 1926. The sign on the building to the right advertises dental services.

To go with his repair shop on Fremont, the Las Vegas Garage, James Down also sold Studebaker cars.

The Hotel Nevada, where the town's first telephone was installed in 1906, shared its first floor for a time with the Bank of Southern Nevada in the 1920s. New owners changed the hotel's name to "Sal Sagev"—Las Vegas spelled backward—in 1928. The business has always enjoyed a good location at Main and Fremont. Renovated and renamed the Golden Gate in the 1960s, it is the city's longest continuously operating hotel.

In 1929, American flags and patriotic bunting decorated the Las Vegas depot of the Union Pacific Railroad, which by then had bought out Clark's shares in the San Pedro, Los Angeles & Salt Lake City Railroad. A direction sign shows the miles required to travel to cities to the east, starting on Main Street.

An officer gets the attention of an airport worker between lines of Army Air Corps planes at Rockwell Field outside Las Vegas in 1929. Sunrise Mountain, directly to the east, is framed between the planes in the background.

Las Vegas resident Maurine Wilson (right) stands beside planes parked at Rockwell Field. Area pilots were called to help with the search for pilot Maury Graham, whose biplane had crashed on January 10, 1930. His body was found six months later. He had flown the first airmail delivery plane from Las Vegas, in 1926.

Hoover Dam, Gaming, and the Early Las Vegas Strip

(1930–1949)

Local public school students, including a couple of Boy Scouts, hold flags and signs during a ceremony for the laying of the cornerstone of Las Vegas High School, the area's first high school not connected to its grammar school, on February 22, 1930.

In a shade of Las Vegas' not-too-distant past, a horse-drawn covered wagon, with people dressed in turn-of-the-century period clothing, rolls past spectators and automobiles on Fremont Street during a Labor Day parade around 1930.

Proud members of the Las Vegas Volunteer Fire Department relax against their motorized fire engine and hose system under shade trees in 1930. The well-respected department remained all volunteer until 1940.

Hundreds of Las Vegas citizens and others, many coming by car and some by bus, cram together in Bracken, Nevada, to hail the dedication of the first laying of railroad track to Hoover Dam, on September 17, 1930. City residents were excited about the benefits to the city the dam's construction would bring. The trains started running to Boulder City in April 1931. Las Vegas would serve as the main hub for supplies for the immense dam project.

Bunting hangs on the Union Pacific railroad station in Las Vegas to celebrate the start of railroad construction, connecting Las Vegas to Boulder City and the dam site in 1930. Union Pacific would build 23 miles of track to Boulder City, and the U.S. government would build 10 miles to the dam site. Later that year, Congress approved funding for the dam, and construction bids were opened on March 4, 1931.

Commemorative decorations adorned the renovated Berkley's men's store downtown on September 15, 1930, two days before the dedication of the new railroad from Las Vegas to Hoover Dam.

Blocks of Fremont Street are awash in American flags and others, which festoon the street in celebration of the railroad to Boulder City in 1930.

Manning a lightened, bare-bones automobile and trailer, these young local men took a road trip to the Colorado River in 1931.

The float made for Sam Gelber's Electric Shop, on top of a car, heads down Fremont Street, about 1930.

Local character Frank Waite ran for sheriff in 1930 and 1934, campaigning in a burro-pulled, small covered wagon that he drove throughout town with his dog. His bid for the office was unsuccessful in both races.

Rapid progress continued in Las Vegas, now with passenger aircraft service in the early 1930s. A Western Air Express plane from Los Angeles has just landed.

The Boulder Club bar and casino figures prominently in this 1930s view of Fremont Street. The club's second floor housed the Union Labor Temple. A store sign (right) announces watermelon for sale.

With the Hoover Dam (then known as Boulder Dam) project under way, Las Vegas city officials decided to build an archway touting its new, national distinction as the "gateway" to Boulder Dam, which began construction in 1931. Marchers walk under the arch during a Labor Day parade in the early 1930s.

Labor union members and friends pose with their float for the Labor Day parade down Fremont Street in the early 1930s.

In the early 1930s, auto dealer James Cashman, left, greets movie actress Loretta Young and Colonel
Roscoe Turner, a well-known aviator and lead pilot for Nevada Airlines. Turner had just arrived at
the new Western Air Express airport in Las Vegas in a Lockheed plane, the Gilmore Lion, owned by
California oil man Earl B. Gilmore. Turner was a favored pilot to the stars and made "alimony special"
flights for would-be divorcees from Los Angeles to Reno in only 3.5 hours.

In 1933, the U.S. government completed this federal building and post office on Stewart Street, two blocks northeast of Fremont Street. The building is currently the site of a planned city museum focusing on organized crime.

Downtown's finest theater was the El Portal, opened in 1928. Seen here in 1934 showing a Shirley Temple movie, the theater, on Fremont between Third and Fourth streets, had 713 seats. For a higher admission price, patrons could sit in a loge section and choose from 84 large leather seats. The former theater survives today as a souvenir shop.

Johnny Roventini, the famous Philip Morris "Johnny the Bellboy," known for his "Call for Philip Morris!" tag line during national radio commercials for the cigarette maker, stands inside a convertible in downtown Las Vegas in 1935, during that year's Helldorado parade. Not widely known at the time was that Roventini had been living in Las Vegas for years. The men to the left are former Nevada lieutenant governor Fred Alward (far left), and Leonard Arnett, a local drugstore owner.

By the mid-1930s, about 300,000 tourists a year were visiting Las Vegas, and the main attraction was Hoover Dam, completed in 1935. In this promotional parade float from that time period, the Las Vegas Chamber of Commerce uses the dam project as proof that Las Vegas had become "the City of an Assured Future."

Half a dozen men and a boy holding the reins of a horse gather at a local horse-race track about three miles outside town, near the present-day Las Vegas Hilton. The scales behind the truck might have been used for weighing jockeys.

In this aerial photograph looking toward Arizona, parked cars line the highway across the top of Hoover Dam after it was completed and dedicated by President Roosevelt on September 30, 1935. The concrete dam was a spectacular achievement in world engineering history. At 1,244 feet long at its crest and 660 feet thick at its base, it is larger than any of Egypt's pyramids. It created the man-made Lake Mead. Water running from the lake through the dam spins turbines to generate electrical power for Southern Nevada and beyond, provides flood control and drinking water for Southern California, and provides irrigation in Arizona.

Facing east on Fremont Street in the mid-1930s. At left, the Overland Hotel promotes itself as "air cooled." True air conditioning (better than so-called swamp coolers, which merely fanned evaporating water) came to Las Vegas around this time and greatly enhanced the future of the city in the Mojave Desert. The Sal Sagev hotel is at right, and farther down the street is the marquee of the Northern Club casino.

The Las Vegas Club, owned by J. Kell Houssels, on Fremont Street in the mid-1930s. The club was originally a pool hall that served soft drinks before Prohibition ended and Nevada permitted casinos. After repeal of prohibition and the legalization of casinos, early club owners like Houssels took advantage of both. He later bought shares of other casinos and in the late 1950s operated the Tropicana Hotel on the Strip.

This mid-1930s west-facing view of Fremont Street toward the Union Pacific depot (center) shows, at left, Berkley's clothing store, the Las Vegas Club, the Northern Club, and Sal Sagev hotel. At right are the Las Vegas Pharmacy, a shoe-shine stand, Ethel's Liquor store, the State Cafe, J. C. Penney store, and the Overland Hotel.

Resting her hands on a washing machine, a woman stands outside the Rockwell Electric Shop, which used a truck for pickups and deliveries in the 1930s.

As Europe prepared for war in the 1930s, many people throughout the United States opposed involvement overseas by the nation's armed forces. The anti-war fervor reached Las Vegas about 1939, when this group of isolationists, including children, demonstrated during a march on Fremont Street. The Japanese bombing of Pearl Harbor in 1941 would alter public opinion dramatically.

Las Vegas' Union Pacific station was used for on-location filming of the aptly named motion picture *Union Pacific* in 1938. Film director Cecil B. DeMille had the train station decorated as if it were in Virginia instead of Nevada. The movie was released in 1939.

Dozens of smartly dressed members of the Las Vegas Rotary Club take time to stand for a photograph on Fremont Street during their Christmas Party in 1940. Seated in the Santa's sleigh-like car, next to a costumed Saint Nick, is club president A. C. Grant.

The Sal Sagev hotel and Fremont Street as they looked in 1940.

The El Rancho Vegas, about four miles south of downtown on the old Los Angeles Highway just outside the city limits, made history in 1941 as the first hotel resort on the Las Vegas Strip. The El Rancho had a unique windmill tower sign. Built by Thomas Hull, a hotelier from California, it featured a pool, three restaurants, and ample parking—for 400 cars.

The Eldorado Club became one of the more popular downtown casinos after it opened in 1947 at Fremont and Second streets, with a separate hotel, the Apache, above it. Closed due to owing back taxes, the Eldorado was sold in 1951 to Benny Binion, who turned it into Binion's Horseshoe Club.

Opened in 1942, the Pioneer (without hotel rooms) was another downtown casino favored by tourists and locals. The Pioneer became best known for the 48-foot-tall neon sign fashioned after a waving cowboy, "Vegas Vic." The moving sign was accompanied for many years by a loud, recorded voice of a man saying, "Howdy partner. Welcome to Las Vegas." Vegas Vic became the symbol of the town for millions of tourists.

The Little Chapel of the West, which opened with the Last Frontier Hotel on the Las Vegas Strip in 1942, is placed on a truck to be moved to a different section of the hotel property in 1954. As was true for other Las Vegas wedding chapels, it would flourish amid Nevada's easy marriage and divorce laws. In 1943, the solid redwood chapel would witness the first of many celebrity couples to marry there—actress Betty Grable and bandleader Harry James. The chapel is still open for business on Russell Road and Las Vegas Boulevard South.

Melting snow made driving hazardous on Fremont Street outside the Overland Hotel, one day in the 1940s.

Two kids sit before a "no parking" zone in front of a liquor store on a sunny day on Fremont Street about 1943.

Fremont Street is seen here clogged with parked cars in the 1940s.

A searchlight highlights the October 30, 1942, opening of the Last Frontier Hotel. Its main attraction was the "Last Frontier Village," an Old West town done up Hollywood style, exhibiting hundreds of vintage western artifacts. The Last Frontier became the second hotel-casino to debut on the fledgling Strip. Owner William J. Moore, trying to outdo the El Rancho, tempted motorists by installing a swimming pool out front. Moore also added a 600-seat banquet facility and parking lots for 900 cars.

The Turf Club bar and casino on Fremont Street in the mid-1940s.

The crew of the *Memphis Belle* B-17 bomber stands beside the famous aircraft at the gunnery school about 1943. The plane was the first to complete 25 American bombing missions over Germany during World War II. Flown to the United States, its crew was sent on tour with the plane to sell war bonds. In July 1943, the *Belle* visited Las Vegas, where three of its crew had trained in the gunnery school. The reference to "Basic Magnesium" in the sign was the Basic Magnesium plant, a factory about 15 miles to the southeast, where magnesium mined in southern Nevada was forged to build airplane parts, thousands of incendiary bombs, and machine-gun tracer bullets used during the war.

Men in uniform (right) cross Second Street at Fremont in the bustling downtown of the early 1940s, when lucrative defense contracts, such as at the gunnery school and Basic Magnesium Inc., created thousands of jobs, bringing new residents and growth. The BMI plant alone created 15,000 wartime jobs.

Last Frontier Hotel owner William J. Moore, who opened the resort on the budding Las Vegas Strip in 1942, waves from a decorated, horse-drawn buggy in his position as "ringmaster" of the Helldorado parade in 1945. Tony Cornero's S. S. Rex Club casino is visible in the background.

The Golden Nugget casino at night.

Post–World War II nuclear bomb tests during the Cold War took place throughout the 1950s at the Nevada Test Site, 65 miles north of Las Vegas. The mushroom cloud of one test, on April 18, 1953, can be seen between these downtown casino signs. Hotel promoters used the scheduled tests as a visitor attraction in the early 1950s. Tourists stayed up until nearly dawn to catch sight of the tests' clouds from hotel rooftops.

Modern Las Vegas Takes Shape

(1950–1959)

The Pioneer Club's large rooftop neon sign, with the head and hand of its Vegas Vic cowboy character, competes with the other gleaming casino signs at night on Fremont.

One of the first off-Strip casinos was the Showboat, with a 100-room hotel sporting a facade fashioned after a Mississippi riverboat. Former *Las Vegas Age* publisher Charles "Pop" Squires is seen here cutting the opening ribbon in 1954. The Showboat, on Boulder Highway near Fremont Street, would eventually prove popular with local gamblers. Its partners included Las Vegas Club owner J. Kell Houssels and Desert Inn hotel executive Moe Dalitz.

A member of the Sands Hotel's chorus line, the Copa Girls, practices her dance moves in front of the hotel on the Strip around 1955. The Sands debuted in 1952, and its popularity defined Las Vegas for many people, especially during its golden years as a top entertainment spot and hub for singers Frank Sinatra, Dean Martin, and Sammy Davis, Jr., throughout the 1950s and 1960s. But as was true for many Las Vegas casinos, organized crime figures held concealed interests in the Sands into the 1960s.

Singer Dean Martin, on stage during his opening night at the Sands' Copa Room, March 6, 1957. Martin seems to be reacting to the celebrities sitting at a front table, including Jack Benny, Desi Arnaz, and Lucille Ball. Martin and his "Rat Pack" friends Sinatra and Davis, would make the Sands internationally famous and become major draws for other Las Vegas casinos into the 1980s.

In 1959, designer Betty Willis
fashioned this famous piece of Las
Vegas neon history, the welcome
sign that still greets motorists at
the Strip's south end.

NOTES ON THE PHOTOGRAPHS

These notes, listed by page number, attempt to include all aspects known of the photographs. Each of the photographs is identified by the page number, a title or description, photographer and collection, archive, and call or box number when applicable. Although every attempt was made to collect all data, in some cases complete data may have been unavailable due to the age and condition of some of the photographs and records.

60 HOTEL NATIONAL
University of Nevada Las
Vegas Libraries, Special
Collections
0090_0009_OS

61 OVERLAND HOTEL
University of Nevada Las
Vegas Libraries, Special
Collections
0013_0003_OS

62 CONKLIN BROTHERS
University of Nevada Las
Vegas Libraries, Special
Collections
0054_0002_OS

63 TEXACO FILLING STATION
University of Nevada Las
Vegas Libraries, Special
Collections
0015_0003_OS

64 NEON SIGNS
University of Nevada Las
Vegas Libraries, Special
Collections
0100_1851_OS

65 APEX FILLING STATION
University of Nevada Las
Vegas Libraries, Special
Collections
0006_0043_OS

66 TEACHERS WITH STUDENTS
University of Nevada Las
Vegas Libraries, Special
Collections
0214_0159_OS

67 FIREPROOF GARAGE
University of Nevada Las
Vegas Libraries, Special
Collections
0054_0001_OS

68 OPEN-AIR CAR
University of Nevada Las
Vegas Libraries, Special
Collections
0214_0001_OS

69 TREES ON FIFTH STREET
University of Nevada Las
Vegas Libraries, Special
Collections
0198_0001_OS

70 HARLEY HARMON ON TRUCK
University of Nevada Las
Vegas Libraries, Special
Collections
0214_0172_OS

71 FREMONT STREET SCENE
University of Nevada Las
Vegas Libraries, Special
Collections
0097_0064_OS

72 OVERLAND HOTEL
University of Nevada Las
Vegas Libraries, Special
Collections
0097_0065_OS

73 FIRST AIR MAIL PLANE
University of Nevada Las
Vegas Libraries, Special
Collections
0008_0077A_OS

74 SPECIAL DELIVERY
University of Nevada Las
Vegas Libraries, Special
Collections
0017_0010_OS

75 FREMONT STREET, 1926
University of Nevada Las
Vegas Libraries, Special
Collections
0002_0214_OS

76 REPAIR SHOP
University of Nevada Las
Vegas Libraries, Special
Collections
0015_0002_OS

77 HOTEL NEVADA
University of Nevada Las
Vegas Libraries, Special
Collections
0204_0048_OS

78 UNION PACIFIC DEPOT
University of Nevada Las
Vegas Libraries, Special
Collections
0204_0049_OS

79 ARMY AIR CORPS PLANES
University of Nevada Las
Vegas Libraries, Special
Collections
0014_0703_OS

80 FEMALE PILOT
University of Nevada Las
Vegas Libraries, Special
Collections
0014_0089_OS

82 LAYING CORNERSTONE
University of Nevada Las
Vegas Libraries, Special
Collections
0265_0226_OS

83 LABOR DAY PARADE
University of Nevada Las
Vegas Libraries, Special
Collections
0020_0020_OS

84 FIRE DEPARTMENT
University of Nevada Las
Vegas Libraries, Special
Collections
0015_0006_OS

85 TRACK TO HOOVER DAM
University of Nevada Las
Vegas Libraries, Special
Collections
0010_0068_OS

86 RAILROAD STATION
University of Nevada Las
Vegas Libraries, Special
Collections
0010_0068_OS

87 BERKLEY'S MEN'S STORE
University of Nevada Las
Vegas Libraries, Special
Collections
0148_0010_OS

88 FREMONT STREET, 1930
University of Nevada Las
Vegas Libraries, Special
Collections
0265_0365_OS

89 BARE-BONES AUTOMOBILE
University of Nevada Las
Vegas Libraries, Special
Collections
0214_0173_OS

90 FLOATS
University of Nevada Las
Vegas Libraries, Special
Collections
0008_0067_OS

91 FRANK WAITE FOR SHERIFF
University of Nevada Las
Vegas Libraries, Special
Collections
0002_0128_OS

92 PASSENGER AIRCRAFT
University of Nevada Las
Vegas Libraries, Special
Collections
0232_0041_OS

93 BOULDER CLUB
University of Nevada Las
Vegas Libraries, Special
Collections
0253_0002_OS

94 ARCHWAY CELEBRATION
University of Nevada Las
Vegas Libraries, Special
Collections
0265_0330_OS

95 LABOR DAY FLOAT
University of Nevada Las
Vegas Libraries, Special
Collections
0265_0336_OS

96 THE GILMORE LION
University of Nevada Las
Vegas Libraries, Special
Collections
0013_0012_OS

Printed in the USA
CPSIA information can be obtained
at www.ICGtesting.com
JSHW072025140824
68134JS00042B/3782

9 781683 368472